KATE MULVANY is an award-winning playwright and screenwriter. Her new play, *The Rasputin Affair*, was shortlisted for the Griffin New Play Award and the Patrick White Award and will premiere at Ensemble Theatre in 2017. Her stage adaptation of Craig Silvey's novel *Jasper Jones* was performed to sold-out crowds at Belvoir in 2016 and 2017, and went on to tour nationally. In 2015, she penned *Masquerade*, a reimagining of the much-loved children's book by Kit Williams, which was performed at the 2015 Sydney Festival, the State Theatre Company of South Australia and the Melbourne Festival. Her autobiographical play, *The Seed*, commissioned by Belvoir, won the Sydney Theatre Award for Best Independent Production in 2007 and is currently being developed into a feature film. Kate's *Medea*, created with Anne-Louise Sarks and produced by Belvoir in 2012, won a number of awards including an AWGIE and five Sydney Theatre Awards. It completed hugely successful seasons at London's Gate Theatre and Auckland's Silo Theatre. She's also currently under commission at Sydney Theatre Company. Kate's other plays and musicals include *The Danger Age* (Deckchair Theatre/La Boite); *Blood and Bone* (The Stables/Naked Theatre Company); *The Web* (Hothouse/Black Swan State Theatre Company); *Somewhere* (co-written with Tim Minchin for the Joan Sutherland PAC); and *Storytime* (Old Fitzroy Theatre), which won Kate the 2004 Philip Parsons Award. Kate is also an award-winning stage and screen actor, whose credits include *The Seed*, *Buried Child* (Belvoir); *Blasted* (B Sharp/Sheedy Productions); *Tartuffe*, *Macbeth*, *Julius Caesar* (Bell Shakespeare); *The Crucible*, *Proof*, *A Man With Five Children*, *King Lear*, *Rabbit* (Sydney Theatre Company); *The Beast* (Melbourne Theatre Company); *The Literati*, *Mr Bailey's Minder* (Griffin Theatre Company); and the feature films *The Little Death* and *The Great Gatsby*.

Nathan O'Keefe as Jack Hare in Griffin Theatre Company and State Theatre Company of South Australia's 2015 production at the Sydney Opera House. (Photo: Brett Boardman)

MASQUERADE

BY KATE MULVANY
BASED ON THE BOOK BY KIT WILLIAMS

Currency Press,
Sydney

CURRENCY PLAYS

First published in 2015
by Currency Press Pty Ltd,
PO Box 2287, Strawberry Hills, NSW, 2012, Australia
enquiries@currency.com.au
www.currency.com.au

in association with Griffin Theatre Company

This revised edition published in 2017

Copyright: Introduction © Kate Mulvany, 2017; *Masquerade* © Kate Mulvany and Kit Williams, 2015.

COPYING FOR EDUCATIONAL PURPOSES

The Australian *Copyright Act 1968* (Act) allows a maximum of one chapter or 10% of this book, whichever is the greater, to be copied by any educational institution for its educational purposes provided that that educational institution (or the body that administers it) has given a remuneration notice to Copyright Agency Limited (CAL) under the Act.

For details of the CAL licence for educational institutions contact CAL, 11/66 Goulburn Street, Sydney, NSW, 2000; tel: within Australia 1800 066 844 toll free; outside Australia 61 2 9394 7600; fax: 61 2 9394 7601; email: info@copyright.com.au

COPYING FOR OTHER PURPOSES

Except as permitted under the Act, for example a fair dealing for the purposes of study, research, criticism or review, no part of this book may be reproduced, stored in a retrieval system, or transmitted in any form or by any means without prior written permission. All enquiries should be made to the publisher at the address above.

Any performance or public reading of *Masquerade* is forbidden unless a licence has been received from the author or the author's agent. The purchase of this book in no way gives the purchaser the right to perform the play in public, whether by means of a staged production or a reading. All applications for public performance should be addressed to Cameron's Management, Locked Bag 848, Surry Hills NSW 2010, Australia; ph: 61 2 9319 7199; info@cameronsmanagement.com.au

Cataloguing-in-publication data for this title is available from the National Library of Australia website: www.nla.gov.au

Typeset by Dean Nottle for Currency Press.
Cover design by Emma Vine.

Currency Press acknowledges the Traditional Owners of the Country on which we live and work. We pay our respects to all Aboriginal and Torres Strait Islander Elders, past and present.

Contents

Introduction
by Kate Mulvany — vii

MASQUERADE

Act One — 1

Act Two — 36

Kate Cheel as the Moon and Mikelangelo as the Sun in Griffin Theatre Company and State Theatre Company of South Australia's 2015 production at the Sydney Opera House. (Photo: Brett Boardman)

Introduction

Welcome! I am all at once honoured, terrified and ecstatic that you are joining the *Masquerade* journey.

And believe me, it has been quite the journey getting this play onto the page and stage...

As a child, the book *Masquerade* was given to me by a very special woman named Tessa. She'd read it to me at my hospital bedside, and together we would dive into Kit Williams' magical world with awestruck wonder.

We'd puzzle over its riddles and clues and we'd convince each other – woman and child – that we would one day solve the mystery of the missing amulet. *Masquerade* made the timelessness of a children's oncology ward somehow bearable.

I survived my childhood illness and even though this world has lost Tessa, her book has remained by my side always. So it was the greatest thrill of my life when, in 2009, I met with the elusive *Masquerade* author Kit Williams and he gave me permission to adapt it into the play you are seeing today – on two conditions: that I include the story of myself and Tessa, and that the play be 'for nine to ninety year olds'.

I am more than aware of the gem I hold in my hands, that you now hold in yours. The story of a hare named Jack who sets off on a celestial journey to deliver a token of love from the Moon to the Sun. A story that inspired millions and set off an international treasure hunt. The story that helped me survive my illness. The journey you have now joined!

There are far too many mortals to thank here. But I am infinitely grateful to everyone that has been part of this story. I would like to single out Kit and Eleyne Williams for trusting this Australian playwright with such a precious gem, and becoming such dear friends along the way, and Sam Strong for his fearless foresight and endless support.

I'm so thrilled you are taking a leap with this beautiful bunch of characters into the unknown. They make wonderful travel companions.

Enjoy the journey.

Kate Mulvany
2017

Nathan O'Keefe as Jack Hare, Helen Dallimore as Tessa, Louis Fontaine as Joe, Pip Branson as the Man Who Plays the Music That Makes the World Go Round and Zindzi Okenyo as Pig in Griffin Theatre Company and State Theatre Company of South Australia's 2015 production at the Sydney Opera House. (Photo: Brett Boardman)

Masquerade was first performed by Griffin Theatre Company and State Theatre Company of South Australia at the Drama Theatre, Sydney Opera House, on 7 January 2015, with the following cast:

TESSA	Helen Dallimore
JACK HARE	Nathan O'Keefe
JOE	Louis Fontaine / Jack Andrew
MOON / TARA TREETOPS	Kate Cheel
NURSE / FAT PIG / DAWN PENNY POCKETS / FISH	Zindzi Okenyo
THE SUN / THE PRACTICAL MAN	Mikelangelo
THE MAN WHO PLAYS THE MUSIC THAT MAKES THE WORLD GO ROUND / SIR ISAAC NEWTON / CRAW	Pip Branson
BARBERS	Guy Freer, Sam Martin, Phil Moriarty

Directors, Lee Lewis & Sam Strong
Designer, Anna Cordingley
Lighting Designer, Geoff Cobham
Composition & Musical Directors, Pip Branson & Mikelangelo
Audio Visual Designer, Chris Petridis
Sound Designer, Michael Toisuta
Assistant Director, Nescha Jelk
Associate Designer, Romanie Harper
Stage Manager, Amy Harris
Music by Mikelangelo and the Black Sea Gentlemen: Mikelangelo, Pip Branson, Guy Freer, Sam Martin, Phil Moriarty

CHARACTERS

JOE, a 10-year-old boy
TESSA, Joe's mother
JACK, a hare
MOON, a raven-haired woman
SUN, a handsome man
THE MAN WHO PLAYS THE MUSIC THAT MAKES THE WORLD GO ROUND, the keeper of time
NURSE, feels nothing
FAT PIG, feels everything
PENNY POCKETS, seller of goods and bads
TARA TREETOPS, collector of dreams
CRAW, a crow
SIR ISAAC NEWTON, a philosopher
THE PRACTICAL MAN, an opportunist
FISH, a fish
DAWN, an early-morning walker
BARBER BOB, BARBER BILL and BARBER BARBARA, an incomplete quartet
MEDICAL STAFF, humourless ghouls
MORTALS, earthbound entities

WRITER'S NOTE

In this play, any one actor will play several different characters. The play was written for five actors and a band of five musicians.

ACT ONE

SCENE ONE

A dark stage.

A young woman appears suddenly. Tries to catch her breath.
She is dressed simply, her clothes rumpled, and looks rather weary. Her name is TESSA.
She tries to regain her composure.
Out of nowhere, a book drops from the sky while TESSA*'s back is turned.*
She picks the book up, a little confused, opens it and reads...

TESSA: 'Within the pages of this book there is a story told
Of love, adventures, fortunes lost, and a jewel of solid gold.
To solve the hidden riddle, you must use your eyes,
And find the hare in every picture that may point you to the prize...'
Huh.

> *The lights fade. As* TESSA *begins to disappear into blackness, a band of* MUSICIANS *begin to play as the stage glows dimly with moonlight...*
>
> TESSA*'s voice continues from the darkness...*

Once upon a perfect night, unclouded and still, there came the face of a pale and beautiful lady.

> *The moonlight glows stronger and a woman appears, cloaked and hooded—the* MOON.

The tresses of her hair reached out to make the constellations...

> *The* MOON *removes her cloak hood and reveals a wild mane of hair that forms a messy orb around her beautiful face. Stars appear in the night sky around her.*

... and the dewy vapours of her gown fell soft upon the land.

> *The* MOON *removes her cloak to reveal a long dress, beautiful and pale.*

Every night she performed her merry dance in the sky...

A violin starts to play a beautiful, lilting melody and THE MOON *begins to dance. As she does, a spotlight reveals a musician—* THE MAN WHO PLAYS THE MUSIC THAT MAKES THE WORLD GO ROUND—*who plays a battered old violin.*

... and depending on the day, the dance took many different forms—waxing and waning, growing from a small sidestep... to a smiling jig... to a full, passionate tango.

During this speech, the MOON *dances as illustrated. At her full point, her dance is seductive and showy—she seems to be performing for someone.*

The lady was most merry in her dance when she knew she was being watched. And the one who watched—from far, far away—was the object of her glowing affection.

From across the stage, a golden light. A MAN *appears from amid the* MUSICIANS—*young and athletic and handsome—*THE SUN. *He watches* THE MOON *intently.* THE MOON *sings, wooing the* SUN *to join in. He does... shyly at first. As he watches, she dances more vibrantly, fully lit. At the height of her dance of seduction she reaches out to him and he smiles brightly. They sing together, growing in volume.*

This lady, whom all mortals call the Moon, had fallen in love with the Sun. However, no matter how happy her dance appeared, it always ended in sadness, for whenever the dance led her into the same part of the sky as the Sun, she seemed to simply fade away.

THE MOON*'s dance begins to wane, despite* THE SUN *beaming at her. His smile fades away. Their singing dwindles away.*

The Sun, on the other hand, contrary to his appearance, was always sad. The one thing he wished for more than anything in the universe was a friend.

The SUN *turns toward* THE MAN WHO PLAYS THE MUSIC THAT MAKES THE WORLD GO ROUND, *who suddenly plays a wrong note and squints as the* SUN *glows brightly in his face.* THE MAN*'s rhythm falters and the music takes on a tuneless quality as he tries to guard his eyes from the* SUN*'s beams.*

But when people looked at the Sun they immediately screwed up their faces and turned away, which made him think that he must be terribly ugly.

The SUN*'s smile fades further and he disappears away, just as the* MOON, *in her weakening dance, reaches out for him.*

Forlornly, the SUN *leaves the stage. The* MOON*'s dance slows further as he departs.*

THE MAN WHO PLAYS THE MUSIC THAT MAKES THE WORLD GO ROUND *recovers his composure and plays again, but the* MOON *does not keep dancing.*

SCENE TWO

A sudden lighting change.

A stern NURSE *opens a curtain. The Celestial World is gone and we are in a cold, white hospital room.*

The NURSE *leaves.*

In a bed is JOE. TESSA *is in the chair beside him—she still holds the book.* JOE *is dressed in pyjamas and a beanie and looks weak and pale.*

JOE: Mum… what's a 'mortal'?
TESSA: Hmm?
JOE: You said, 'This lady, who all mortals call the Moon'.
TESSA: I said no such thing.
JOE: I'll bet you a walk outside that you said, 'This lady, who all mortals call the Moon'.
TESSA: A walk outside?
JOE: A walk outside.

She smiles at him.

TESSA: Even though a walk outside would be nice, what I actually said was, 'This lady, *whom* all mortals call the Moon'.
JOE: That's not fair!
TESSA: Sorry. You lost the bet.
JOE: That's completely unfair!
TESSA: No—that's grammar.
JOE: All because of one letter!

TESSA: You won't get anywhere in this world if you speak like an uneducated frog, Joe.

JOE: But I haven't been outside for days.

> *Beat.*

TESSA: Weeks, actually. But we'll be out of here soon. We just have to wait for your final test results.

> *Beat.*

JOE: So what's a 'mortal'?

> *Beat.*

TESSA: A 'mortal' is a human being. Mortals have eyes and ears and hearts and brains. They live. However, 'mortal' comes from the word 'mort'. 'Mort' means death. So mortals, although needing to be alive to be called such a thing, are also, paradoxically, going to someday die. Mortals.

> *Beat.*

JOE: What did the Moon do when she lost her Sun, Mum?

TESSA: Well, she called upon her hare.

JOE: Her hair?

> *He puts his hand under his beanie.*

TESSA: Not that hair.

> *Beat.*

You're doing very well with that, by the way.

JOE: Thanks.

TESSA: You're welcome.

> *She continues with her story.*

At the end of her dance, as the Sun turned in shame and the Moon faded away, she called out—in her beautiful, ethereal, velvet voice—for her hare.

> *The* MOON *screams piercingly.*

MOON: *Jack!*

> JOE *covers his ears and looks to his mother in shock. She shrugs.*

TESSA: Artistic licence.

Helen Dallimore as Tessa and Louis Fontaine as Joe in Griffin Theatre Company and State Theatre Company of South Australia's 2015 production at the Sydney Opera House. (Photo: Brett Boardman)

SCENE THREE

Back in the Celestial World.

MOON: *Jack! Jack Hare!*

> THE MAN WHO PLAYS THE MUSIC THAT MAKES THE WORLD GO ROUND *noodles softly on his violin in the corner.*

I know you're around here somewhere, Jack. Stop hiding and come out. I need you to run an errand.

> *Still nothing.*

Jack Hare, if you do not come out, I will find you, smack you, then chop off your paws and use them as lucky charms!

> JACK HARE, *brown and furry with enormous ears and alert, wide eyes, emerges, bustling via the* MUSICIANS *and their instruments into* THE MAN WHO PLAYS THE MUSIC THAT MAKES THE WORLD GO ROUND *who loses his song once more…*

JACK: Please don't be chopping me paws off, mistress. I need 'em for so many things.

MOON: Jack, I have an errand for / you.

JACK: [*to the audience*] I pass the salt with them, I put me favourite records on with them, I scratch me bum with / them—

MOON: Jack.

JACK: [*to the audience*] I simply don't know what I'd do without me paws.

MOON: Jack!

> *She takes his paws and caresses them gently.*

I need you to run an errand.

JACK: Yes, mistress Moon. As is my honourable duty.

> *He bows extravagantly.*

MOON: Good. But before you do, I must tell you something important, Jack. Lately I have been consumed by feelings.

> *She strokes his paws softly.* JACK *starts to quiver, his leg thwapping slightly.*

JACK: Sorry. Nervous twitch.

MOON: Feelings growing inside my chest. Feelings new and strange and wonderful.

She places his paw upon her chest.

Do you feel that, Jack?

JACK *seems a little taken aback.*

JACK: Goodness … I do, mistress. It's hurting my paw, actually.
MOON: I have fallen in love, Jack.
JACK: What's that?
MOON: Love.
JACK: Huh?
MOON: Love. Fallen. I've fallen.
JACK: Did you hurt yourself?
MOON: Pardon?
JACK: When you fell.
MOON: No. I've fallen in *love*.
JACK: In lah…

He struggles to say the word

MOON: Love.
JACK: In loo…
MOON: In *love*.
JACK: Laaaaaahhhhrrrr? Quite a tongue twister, isn't it?
MOON: *Love!*

She clutches at his paw again. His quivering intensifies. His hind leg starts to shake even more.

Jack, I need you to go to the Sun…

JACK*'s leg stops shaking.*

JACK: The Sun?

He points at the SUN.

The one that lives all the way over there?

MOON: Yes. And I want you to give him a token of my affection. But first we must ask The Man Who Plays the Music That Makes the World Go Round to slow his playing so that I may gather the materials for my gift.
JACK: But he's the man who plays the music that makes the world go

round. If he stops playing, you know what will happen—
MOON: He won't stop! Just slow down a little.

THE MOON whispers into the ear of THE MAN WHO PLAYS THE MUSIC THAT MAKES THE WORLD GO ROUND. He shakes his head—no. THE MOON *tries again, crossly.* THE MAN *obediently slows his playing.*

Lighting, sound and movement illustrate the following...

TESSA: From the clouds, the Moon plucked a most brilliant-coloured moonstone. From the sea she collected a bright blue sapphire. From the fire of a volcano she took a ruby. And from the earth's green fields she scooped an enormous emerald. Next, with a little gold taken from the dawn sky, she cunningly wrought a splendrous jewel that was the perfect mirror of her love. It had about it a beauty that mocked Time forever.

A glittering amulet in the shape of a hare appears in the MOON*'s hands.* THE MAN WHO PLAYS THE MUSIC THAT MAKES THE WORLD GO ROUND *starts playing again. The* MOON *presents the amulet to* JACK.

MOON: Jack Hare, listen well. I entrust you with this amulet and you have but one day to deliver it to my lord the Sun.
JACK: *One* day?! [*To us*] One fuzzing day!
MOON: From now until I dance again. One day.
JACK: Do you know how far away the Sun is, my lady Moon? A gazillion billion trillion hundred-and-eleventeen miles away. Approximately.
MOON: Love is impatient, Jack.
JACK: Mistress, be careful. We all know what happens when you get impatient. The world goes crazy.

He looks at the amulet.

And what's this? This is a hare! Just like me! Why would you give the Sun a jewel that looks like me?
MOON: I don't know. It was the first thing I thought of. I suppose I just needed a muse.
JACK: [*to us*] Well, we all need a laugh sometimes.

He thinks this is hilarious.

MOON: Jack, to reach the Sun you must travel through earth and air and fire and water. When you reach him, show him the jewel and tell him it will be his if he will only give me the answer to this riddle:

She sings:

> Fifty is my first,
> Nothing is my second,
> Five just makes my third,
> My fourth a vowel is reckoned.
> Now to find my name,
> Fit my parts together,
> I die if I get cold,
> But never fear cold weather.

Have you got that?
JACK: Yes. I'm not stupid.
MOON: Well, your brain is rather small, Jack. Everyone knows that about hares.
JACK: My brain is not small. It's sensibly compact.
MOON: It's important that you remember the riddle, Jack. This is a mission of love.
JACK: I still don't know what that word / means.
MOON: Now go.
JACK: Right. I'll just have a quick pint of cider and then I'll—
MOON: *Go!*

A cacophony of sound as JACK *hurriedly puts the amulet in his satchel and takes off on his journey.* THE MAN WHO PLAYS THE MUSIC THAT MAKES THE WORLD GO ROUND *plays vigorously.* JACK *repeats the riddle to the best of his ability ...*

JACK: Fifty is my first,
> Can't remember the second,
> Something makes my third,
> Oh, I'm in trouble now, I reckon.
> Gotta find the name,
> Pull yourself together,
> I must be getting old.
> Oh, wait! Now I remember!!

Fifty is my first,
Nothing is my second,
Five just makes my third,
My fourth a vowel is reckoned.
Now to find my name,
Fit my parts together,
I die if I get cold,
But never fear cold weather.

SCENE FOUR

The cacophony ends abruptly and we are back in the hospital.

JOE: Why a riddle? He should just say, 'The Moon loves you', and give the Sun the jewel.

TESSA: I'm not sure Jack knows what love is.

JOE: He's not the only one.

TESSA: Besides, love is the most difficult and courageous journey any creature can take and it deserves a good riddle to make sure it is properly requited.

JOE: Love. Pfft. Soppy.

TESSA: Shall I stop telling the story then?

JOE: No. Just… Remember I'm only ten. I don't think I'll understand love until I'm at least eleven and three quarters.

TESSA: Very well.

  JOE *retches suddenly. He holds his stomach and groans in agony.*

JOE: Mum…

  TESSA *holds him close. He clings to her.*

TESSA: It's come back? The pain? I thought it had gone.

JOE: Mum, make it stop. Please!

TESSA: I can't, darling. I'm so sorry. Be strong for me.

JOE: I'm sick of being strong!

  JOE *cries in agony.*

TESSA: Just breathe it through, Joe. Breathe it through. The only job you have in this world is to just keep breathing…

JOE / JACK: I… don't… want… this… job…

ACT ONE 11

As JOE *breathes in and out in pain,* TESSA *finds the nurse's buzzer and presses it. A bell jangles and we are back with* JACK, *whose panting matches the sound of* JOE'*s breathing…*

SCENE FIVE

JACK *is racing around the stage. As he does, he sings.*

JACK: Oh, why does it fall to me, you see?
It always falls on my back,
When there's so many others who be, you see,
Who are much better choices of Jack.

There's that nimble Jack who is so quick
If reports are to be believed,
He can jump a burning candlestick
And make it home by tea.

And little Jack Horner's not doing a lot
But sticking his thumb in a pie,
If he's such a good boy then the little grot
Should give this errand a try.

But it's always me, always me, always me—Jack Hare,
Jack Hare, do this,
Jack Hare do that,
It's really quite unfair.

There's that big show-off, Jack of All Trades,
Why doesn't she ever use him?
And Jack of Hearts and Jack of Spades,
Jack Spratt and Jack O Lantern?

And what about Jack that fell down that hill?
At least he could take a friend,
His head's much better now, and so is Jill's—
Get them to run this errand.

But it's always me, always me, always me—Jack Hare,
Jack Hare, do this,
Jack Hare do that,
It's really very unfair.

Jumping Jack Flash and Jack in the Box,
Has anyone checked if they're free?
Jackanapes, Jackal, Jackass and Jackdaw,
This journey is making me queasy.

Get Union Jack! He's used to it!
He has to stake his claim!
Lumberjack, Flapjack, or even a John,
We need not quibble on names.

But it's always me, always me, always me—Jack Hare,
Jack Hare, do this,
Jack Hare do that,
It's really bloody unfair!

Jack Hare Jack Hare Jack Hare Jack Hare,
Get Jack to do it for me!
And if he doesn't he'd best beware,
I'll kick him up the jacksie

Jack Hare Jack Hare Jack Hare Jack Hare,
Jack Hare won't mind a bit,
Well let me make you very aware
This hare does give a jacksh—

Suddenly, JACK *bumps into an enormously tall woman—*PENNY POCKETS.

PENNY: Language!

JACK *is stopped in his tracks. He looks up at the looming woman. She wears a long buffeted dress with multiple pockets, filled with paraphernalia—candy canes, beads, pinwheels. In her hand she holds a large jar of honey.*

Were you about to swear, little man?

JACK: No. Well, yes… but…

PENNY *grabs* JACK *and squeezes his cheeks roughly. He opens his mouth and she drips some honey on his tongue.* JACK *smacks his lips together.*

PENNY: There. Honey should soothe that hot tongue, trashy tonsils. Now, long ears, a penny for your fortune.

Zindzi Okenyo as Penny Pockets and Nathan O'Keefe as Jack Hare in Griffin Theatre Company and State Theatre Company of South Australia's 2015 production at the Sydney Opera House. (Photo: Brett Boardman)

JACK: I've no penny, miss.
PENNY: *No penny?!* Then why go bumping into people? Have you no manners as well as a filthy, furry farynx?
JACK: I… I just want to know which way to the Sun, please.
PENNY: That's quite a question for a penniless rabbit to ask.
JACK: Hare.

> PENNY *pours honey onto* JACK*'s face.*

PENNY: Clever trousers.
JACK: Knickerbockers!

> PENNY *gasps and pours more honey into* JACK*'s mouth.*

PENNY: If you've no penny then you must answer this riddle.

> PENNY *sings.*
>
>> I have a little house,
>> Its windows number plenty,
>> It's full of flowers that no man picked,
>> You may have it when it's empty.
>
> JACK *looks pleased.*

JACK: Well, that's easy!

> *He stands on his tiptoes and whispers in* PENNY*'s ear.*

SCENE SIX

Back in the hospital. JOE *looks weary from his bout of pain.* TESSA *strokes his hair.*

JOE: I don't get it.
TESSA: Me neither.

> *A voice over a loudspeaker fills the hospital cubicle: the* NURSE. *At some point during the following speech, the* NURSE *enters.*

NURSE: [*over loudspeaker*] It's quite simple, really. The prognosis is not looking good. Joe's haemoglobin count is exceedingly low, despite our efforts. He isn't eating. The vinicristin doesn't seem to be working and the overall thingamijig has increased to a potentially whatsamacallit level. You'll have to start gobbledigooking your 'other options'. Palliative care may be next on the cards, but until

ACT ONE

then, the dactinomycin, flibbertijibbets and rhubarb, rhubarb, rhubarb will be our best hope.

TESSA: Wait. I'm sorry… I thought he was doing well. I thought we were finally getting out of here—

NURSE: Of course, if you could afford the right medicine we'd be able to give it to him. Can you?

TESSA looks confused.

TESSA: Can I what?

NURSE: Afford the right medicine?

TESSA: I thought he *was* on the right medicine.

NURSE: He's on *a* medicine. Not *the* medicine. Can you afford the *right* medicine?

TESSA: Um… no. But I'm trying. We're doing this alone, you see, and I don't want to leave him all by him—

NURSE: Then the best we can hope for is that his final treatment goes well. We'll just have to make it extra extra extra stringent. Agreed?

TESSA: Well… if you say so.

NURSE: Dr Williams to oncology for some extra extra extra stringent medicine please.

JOE hides under the blankets. The NURSE leaves. TESSA sees JOE hiding and rifles through her bag. She gets out some honeycomb and offers it to JOE's huddled figure.

TESSA: Would you like some?

No response.

You really should eat something, Joe. It'll help you stay awake. And I don't want you to sleep while the sun is shining.

A moment of realisation…

Strangely enough… it might just help you with that riddle.

She places it under the blankets. A beat. JOE emerges, licking the honeycomb.

JOE: [*sung*] I have a little house,
 Its windows number plenty…

PENNY: [*offstage*] It's full of flowers that no man picked,
 And you may have it when it's empty.

As JOE *understands the riddle,* PENNY *appears in the Celestial World.*

JACK / JOE: Honeycomb?

SCENE SEVEN

Lighting and sound—back to JACK *and* PENNY. *He is still whispering in her ear.* PENNY *looks stunned.*

PENNY: Correct!

JACK: Now, which way to the Sun?

> PENNY *takes her hand from her pocket and points up. As she does, a squealing figure swoops past her hand and they all duck and scream. The figure disappears.* PENNY *stands and tries to direct* JACK *again, and the figure rushes past again, squealing. As she flits past again and again,* PENNY *attempts to swat her but is pecked by a large crow that sits on the figure's hat. Finally, the figure* [TARA TREETOPS] *hovers above* PENNY *and* JACK *and grins broadly, a sack over her shoulder, a dandelion in her hand. Her crow* [CRAW] *is huge and black.*

TARA: Sorry! Bit windy up there today!

> *A whoosh of wind knocks them all about.*

Hello, there, furry pants.

JACK: They're knickerbockers.

TARA: My name's Tara. Tara Treetops. Tara's from the Latin, you know. It means 'earth'. Isn't that wonderful?

> *A whoosh of wind knocks them around again.*

And this is my friend Craw.

CRAW: Craw! Craw!

TARA: Craw means—

CRAW: Handsome! Handsome!

TARA: What's your name?

JACK: Jack.

TARA: Jack. Gracious!

JACK: Did I do something wrong?

TARA: No—your name. Jack. It means 'gracious'. From the Hebrew.

ACT ONE

CRAW: Hebrew! Hebrew!
JACK: Goodness.
CRAW: Gracious!

> PENNY *sighs impatiently.*

TARA: And your name, madam?
PENNY: You know my name, Tara. It's Penny Pockets. And I know what it means.
TARA: Penelope. From the Greek. Meaning…
PENNY: Money. 'Penny' means coin. Which means money. Which means payment. I was about to tell this rabbit—
JACK: Hare.
PENNY: —his fortune and you've just swooped in and bungled my sale. Payment, please.
TARA: I have no money. I'm Tara Treetops.
CRAW: No money!
PENNY: You're a fruit loop, that's what you are.

> *She turns to* JACK.

Payment.
JACK: I have no money either. I'm just a humble servant. All I have is this jewel!

> *He gets the amulet from his satchel.*

> PENNY *snatches the amulet from him and studies it closely with her sticky honeyed fingers. Everyone is silenced by its beauty.*

PENNY: This will do nicely. Now I'll be on my way.
JACK: But you can't have that, Miss Penny Pockets. It's a token of 'lahhh'… oh, bugger it. Anyway, my mistress Moon has given me the task of delivering it to the Sun. I was simply asking for directions, not my fortune. I don't think I even want to know my fortune. Probably involves a *ragout*. Ah, but listen to me, rabbiting on… I just want to get to the Sun to give him this from my mistress the Moon so she stops acting so strangely and everything is right in the world.

> TARA *is sobbing.*

TARA: That's the most beautiful story I've ever heard.

She blows her nose and there's a whoosh of wind.

The Moon has fallen in love with the Sun!
JACK: *That's* the word. It was right on the tip of my whiskers—
TARA: Give him back the amulet, Penny Pockets.
PENNY: No.
TARA: You'd dare stand in the way of true love?
PENNY: A woman's got to earn a living.
TARA: Penny Pockets—
PENNY: Tara Treetops.
TARA: I'm only going to say it one more time—
PENNY: I'm shaking in my sandals—
TARA: Give Jack back the amulet.
PENNY: No. It's mine now.

A beat. TARA *smiles sweetly. Then…*

TARA: Very well. Sic 'em, Craw!
CRAW: Sic 'em! Sic 'em!

In a flurry of movement, CRAW *attacks* PENNY *to retrieve the amulet.*

The attack takes quite some time. CRAW *finally retrieves the amulet, and leaves* PENNY *covered in honey and black feathers in a heap on the ground before giving the amulet back to* JACK, *who puts it in his satchel.* PENNY *starts to crawl away.*

TARA: Bye, Penny! Have a wonderful day!

PENNY *mumbles and spits feathers as she crawls away.*

JACK: Thank you, very much, Miss Treetops. Thank you, Craw.
CRAW: Pleasure, treasure!

CRAW *puffs himself up and stands proud and handsome.*

JACK: Miss Treetops, if your name means 'earth', then why are you up in the sky?
TARA: We're looking for lost dreams. They're all up there in the clouds and when the clouds become too full the dreams fall down again: the nasty ones as hailstorms and the glorious ones as gentle showers and rainbows.
JACK: Wow… what a fuzzinating job! Looking for lost dreams!

ACT ONE

TARA: Sometimes. Most lost dreams are quite boring though—that's why they're lost. No-one wants to hold onto them.

JACK: Like what?

TARA: Bishops' dreams of corduroy trousers, and swimwear for prime ministers. Bor-ing! Sometimes I'm lucky enough to find the feasts of shipwrecked sailors or the cures of malignant maladies, but not today, I'm afraid. Hey… have you lost a dream? I can try and find it for you if you like.

JACK: No, miss. I've got my dream well and truly here beneath my fur.

TARA: Really? What is it?

JACK: I want to find the Sun.

TARA: Well, I can take you in the right direction. But first… you must hear my riddle.

JACK: I'm all ears.

TARA sings:

TARA: I have a little sister
In the fields she's seen,
Dressed in yellow petticoats
And gown of green,
She's not a bird and cannot sing
But she can fly without a wing.

JACK: That's easy!

He leans in to TARA *and whispers in her ear. She smiles and takes* JACK*'s hand.*

TARA: Now, jump with me and you may find the Sun behind a cloud. Ally-oop!

As they jump into the air, the scene shifts to JOE *and* TESSA *in the hospital.*

SCENE EIGHT

JOE: What does *that* riddle mean?

TESSA is holding a dandelion orb.

TESSA: Make a wish.

JOE: What's the point? I'll still be here.

Sam Martin on double bass, Kate Cheel as Tara Treetops, Helen Dallimore as Tessa, Phil Moriarty on accordion and Louis Fontaine as Joe in Griffin Theatre Company and State Theatre Company of South Australia's 2015 production at the Sydney Opera House. (Photo: Brett Boardman)

ACT ONE

JOE rolls over and faces the wall. TESSA's smile fades. She reaches out to JOE and strokes his head softly.

TESSA: Not long now, Joe. One more treatment and you'll be better. I know it.

The NURSE appears nearby with a trolley of syringes, which she starts to prepare.

TESSA kisses JOE's head.

You be brave, now.

TESSA goes back to the book.

As she does, the lights snap back onto JACK's world. He is in the sky with TARA, looking for THE SUN. Across the stage, THE MOON watches eagerly.

In order to see the progress of her servant Jack, the lady Moon was disregarding all advice given to her by the other celestial bodies, along with Newton's Universal Law of Gravitation. Instead of continuing her dance in her prescribed orbit, she had stayed behind to watch with anticipation the progress of her little servant Jack.

From behind a cloud, the SUN appears and, for a moment, the MOON is caught in the full glow of his rays. They stare at each other, wide-eyed. THE MAN enters and sees them.

In the hospital, JOE turns to his mother.

JOE: So they can see each other—the Moon and the Sun?

TESSA: I'm afraid so.

JOE: What do you mean? That's good, isn't it?

TESSA: Newton's laws of the universe are Newton's Laws of the Universe. Some rules are not to be broken, even where love is involved.

JOE: Who is this Newton and how he gets to make all the laws?

TESSA: Not all of them. He left some room for a little bit of magic. Now make a wish.

THE MAN: You're not supposed to be in that part of the sky!

TESSA: Shush! I want to see what happens!

Beat. JACK takes a deep breath as he faces the dandelion…

SCENE NINE

Back in the Celestial World, the MOON *and the* SUN *sing a riddle. As they do, the bordering letters of the stage start to take form. The music becomes more menacing.*

MOON: I am the beginning of eternity…

> *The letter 'E' appears.*

SUN: Followed by half a circle…

> *A 'C' appears.*

MOON: Close on by half a square…

> *An 'L' glows.*

SUN: Through my fourth my fifth is seen…

> *'IV' and 'V'—the 'V' vanishes, leaving the letter 'I'.*

MOON: To be the first in every pair…

> *The word 'PAIR' is formed—the 'AIR' drops away to leave the 'P'.*

SUN: My sixth begins my seventh…

> *The 'S' is highlighted in both words and remains as the other letters fade away.*

MOON: The end of time and space…

> *The same as before, only this time an 'E' is left.*

SUN / MOON: Now put my parts together to see what's taken place.

> *The letters form the word 'ECLIPSE'.*
>
> *As the* SUN *and the* MOON *are about to meet, the* MEDICAL STAFF *enter the hospital cubicle.*
>
> *The music becomes weird and demonic.*
>
> JOE *shakes his head in panic. He tries to get out of bed.* TESSA *holds him down as the* NURSE *gets out a needle and injects the little boy.*
>
> JOE *screams.*

The worlds are suddenly chaos.

TESSA yells her story as she holds JOE down. He struggles against her.

TESSA: When the Moon realised what her impatience had done, and saw Jack Hare falling out of the sky, she opened her mouth and *screamed*. A horrible, silent, ghostly scream.

THE MOON screams silently. JOE screams loudly.

All the horrors of the night came forth in this one dreadful scream.

Rodents, snakes, bugs and fish litter the stage and the sounds of human voices and clanging and banging ring out. Their terrified silhouettes appear against the night sky.

Because their impatient Moon had broken the Rules of the Universe, all of the Mortals of the Earth were making a fearful din because it was the only way they could think of to be heard. And all the animals ran round and round until they turned into one huge zoological pudding!

As JOE continues to be injected, the following chant is heard from the MORTALS and/or the MEDICAL STAFF.

MORTALS / STAFF: A hopper of ditches,
    A cropper of corn,
    A little brown deer
    With leathery horn…

TESSA yells intermittently as she holds down her son…

TESSA: What can I do? Is there anything I can *do*? Please tell me what I should do!

MORTALS / STAFF: A hopper of ditches!
    A cropper of corn!
    A little brown deer
    With leathery horn!

JOE: Make it stop! Please make it stop!

MORTALS / STAFF: *A hopper of ditches!*
    A cropper of corn!
    A little brown deer
    With leathery horn!

As the MEDICAL STAFF *finally leave, the din dies and the only sounds that remain are* JOE *weeping and the sorrowful tune coming from the violin of* THE MAN WHO PLAYS THE MUSIC THAT MAKES THE WORLD GO ROUND.

TESSA strokes her son's head lovingly as she sings the first riddle softly...

TESSA: Fifty is my first,
Nothing is my second,
Five just makes my third,
My fourth a vowel is reckoned…

TESSA is exhausted. JOE *is quivering.*

JOE: Mum… why do you let them do that to me?
TESSA: It's for your own good, Joe. I promise.

She goes to hug him. He shoves her away roughly.

TESSA is stunned.

She sadly opens the book again and continues reading softly.

Now that the eclipse had passed, Jack decided to continue his journey, but then he heard the strains of a sad and sorrowful tune…

SCENE TEN

JACK *rouses and carefully approaches* THE MAN WHO PLAYS THE MUSIC THAT MAKES THE WORLD GO ROUND. *After a moment,* THE MAN *notices* JACK.

THE MAN: Good day. I am The Man Who Plays the Music That Makes the World Go Round.
JACK: That's the longest name I've ever heard.
THE MAN: Yes. Makes it very tricky to fill out my tax forms.

THE MAN *smiles.* JACK *stares at him.*

TESSA *speaks from the hospital.*

TESSA: Jack couldn't stop looking at the man's face, for he was the most curiously peculiar creature Jack had ever seen.
JACK: [*to the audience*] Except for an eighty-three-year-old tortoise at the Dudley Zoo.

ACT ONE

THE MAN: Can I help you?

TESSA: Jack related his story—the Moon and the Sun, the word he didn't quite understand, the riddle, the amulet, Penny Pockets and Tara Treetops, the strange darkness that overtook the land, the world going crazy…

> JACK *enacts it all in quick-time.*

THE MAN: I am but a poet and a musician. In my opinion, you require the assistance of the Practical Man. You must go to the town and seek him out.

JACK: Right! I'll just have a quick pint of cider and then I'll—

THE MAN: Go!

> THE MAN WHO PLAYS THE MUSIC THAT MAKES THE WORLD GO ROUND *plays a song.*

TESSA: The Man Who Plays the Music That Makes the World Go Round began to play the sweet song of the Sun, so the day's eyes opened again. The darkness cleared, the dandelions bloomed and Jack set off to the nearest town. Unfortunately, because the weather was so unexpectedly brilliant, all of the shopkeepers put up their closed signs and went to the beach, and Jack couldn't find anyone to ask for directions to the Practical Man.

SCENE ELEVEN

JACK *calls out to the audience.*

JACK: Pardon me! Have you seen the Prodigal Man?

> *He tries again.*

I'm looking for the Pragmatic Man. Have you seen him? Anyone?

> *Another.*

The Proverbial Man? Pardon me? Do you know the Probiscus Man?

> *A rotund man in glasses pops his head out of the door of an antique shop. It is the* PRACTICAL MAN.

Excuse me! I'm looking for the… the Priest… the President… the Proctologist…

PRACTICAL MAN: The Practical Man?

JACK: That's him! Is that you?

PRACTICAL MAN: Well, on Friday afternoons I could be practically anything! Would you like to come in? I have many treasures of antiquity that will take your fancy, or maybe I can show you a hare-loom or two?

The PRACTICAL MAN *laughs uproariously.*

JACK: [*to the audience*] Oh no. A humourist.

PRACTICAL MAN: Step inside.

They do.

JACK: [*to the* PRACTICAL MAN] I'm in quite a hurry, sir. I have to get to the Sun, you see. My mistress has fallen in loh… in lee… in loo…

PRACTICAL MAN: In love? She's fallen in love?

JACK: That's the word. Yes. And so to show the Sun she has fallen in…

PRACTICAL MAN: Love.

JACK: She has collected all of the most beautiful thingamijigs in the world and made it into this whatchamacallit that I have to take to the Sun. I wish she'd used a bit less gold though. It's a heavy little bugger.

PRACTICAL MAN: Gold, you say?

JACK: Twenty-four carats!

PRACTICAL MAN: Really? May I see it? Being a purveyor of the finest thingamijigs and whatchamacallits it would give me great pleasure to view such a piece.

JACK *grins and gives the amulet to the* PRACTICAL MAN *who gets out his glasses to view the jewel.*

JACK: What do you think, Mr Practical Man?

PRACTICAL MAN: It is indeed the finest jewel I have ever seen.

Beat.

I can take you to the Sun.

JACK: Really?

JACK *gets the amulet from the* PRACTICAL MAN*'s grip.*

PRACTICAL MAN: Yes. But we must be quick. Dusk is on its way. And you know what that means… teatime!

He gets a magnifying glass out of his pocket and holds it over the driftwood. A tiny spot of light appears.

Do you see that, Jack? Here he is! The Sun!
JACK: Really? [*To us*] Goodness, he's much smaller than I thought he'd be.
PRACTICAL MAN: Just wait. He'll get bigger. Get closer and you'll see. And then it will be time for tea.

JACK gets closer. The fire sparks and a small flame appears. As he bends over, the PRACTICAL MAN sprinkles salt on JACK's tail.

JACK: Wow! Hallo, My lord the Sun! I have something for you from my mistress the Moon!

The flame grows larger. Unseen by JACK, the PRACTICAL MAN gets out a toasting fork.

The PRACTICAL MAN raises the toasting fork threateningly.

A bearded man eating an apple enters the scene and watches on with horror. It is SIR ISAAC NEWTON.

In slow motion the PRACTICAL MAN spikes JACK in his bottom with the fork. JACK leaps high in the air and down toward the fire as the PRACTICAL MAN tucks a napkin into his collar and catches JACK's satchel. SIR ISAAC raises his hands and splays his fingers and gives an almighty gravitational pull. As he does, JACK flies away from the fire and over the PRACTICAL MAN's head. As he passes, JACK grabs the satchel and lands beside SIR ISAAC. SIR ISAAC glares at the PRACTICAL MAN, who runs away screaming.

SCENE TWELVE

JACK: Thank you! You saved me from having my fur fried! How did you do that?
SIR ISAAC: Well, I am Sir Isaac Newton. I simply grabbed the strings of gravitational force that bound you to your destiny and I pulled.
JACK: Huh! Simple as that, hey?
SIR ISAAC: Indeed.
JACK: I'm looking for the Sun. Do you know him?
SIR ISAAC: We've crossed paths a couple of times.

JACK: My destiny is to give him this amulet for my mistress the Moon. She's in 'loo...', in 'laaah...', in 'li...'
SIR ISAAC: Ahhh. Love.
JACK: That's the word. Anyway, she's asked me to deliver this to him. But I'm afraid he's not going to hang around much longer and I'm running out of time. Do you think you could pull on the gravitational strings again and take me to him?
SIR ISAAC: I'm afraid not. You see, your destiny involves earth, air, fire and water. You've got the earth bit covered, you've been up in the air, you've touched the fire, but you haven't had any water yet.
JACK: I'm not a fan of water. Makes my fur go spiky.
SIR ISAAC: Life's tough.

> SIR ISAAC *pulls on the strings again and* JACK *falls—SPLASH—into the sea.*

SCENE THIRTEEN

JACK *falls and swims and paddles and floats and somersaults, immersed by the blue water. In the distance, a yellow light appears.*

JACK: This must surely be the Sun!

> *The golden light makes its way through the blue water toward* JACK. *It is a* FISH.

FISH: Glood day.
JACK: Oh, I thought you were the Sun.
FISH: How abslurd! Why have you come to the blottom of the ocean?
JACK: Please, oh fish, most worthy, noble and glorious...
FISH: And educated.
JACK: Pardon?
FISH: I just came from my school.

> *He laughs uproariously.* JACK *just rolls his eyes.*

JACK: Could you please direct me to the Sun before the day disappears? My mistress is in loooo... in laaaaah...
FISH: Love?
JACK: Whatever that means.
FISH: In that clase, I will help you if you can blanswer this riddle:

He sings:

> What is nothing on its outside
> And nothing on its inside,
> Is lighter than a fleather,
> But ten men cannot pick it up?

SCENE FOURTEEN

In the hospital, TESSA *blows bubbles. They fill the cubicle.*

JOE: That's silly. Anything that's lighter than a feather can be picked up. Especially by ten men. But how can it be anything if it's nothing?

TESSA: Hmm. Well, let's see.

She blows more bubbles.

> What is nothing on the outside…
> And nothing on the inside…
> Is lighter than a feather…
> But ten men cannot pick it up?

JOE / JACK: A bubble!

SCENE FIFTEEN

JACK *is still swimming beside the* FISH. *He opens his mouth and out comes a bubble.*

FISH: Correct! Now, here are your instructions. Stand at the water's edge and you will see a golden path appear upon the sea. If you can run its length before the Sun sets, you will reach your destination. Glood luck!

JACK swims to the surface of the water and gasps for air—as does JOE—*and leaps onto the shore. He begins to run.*

TESSA: Already the golden light of late afternoon was colouring the sky, and Jack realised that time was desperately short. He began running as fast as his legs would carry him until he reached the golden path that was forming on the surface of the sea.

The SUN *is beginning to set and his golden glow has cast a glittering path across the surface of the sea.*

JACK: The golden path that will take me to the Sun! Wait, Sun! I have something for you! *Wait for me!*

He starts to take a run-up. SIR ISAAC *raises his gravitational strings.* JACK *pulls.* SIR ISAAC *pulls back.* JACK *pulls harder.*

SIR ISAAC: But Jack! No-one has ever run the golden path!

JACK: Oy! Stop pulling me gravitational strings!

SIR ISAAC struggles to keep him on shore.

TESSA: Jack's little hairy legs travelled so speedily and reached such a velocity that no matter how hard Sir Isaac Newton pulled on the hare's gravitational strings, he was forced to let him go.

Finally, JACK *breaks the strings' pull and takes an almighty leap.*

SIR ISAAC: *Jack Hare! No!*

JACK *stands before the* SUN*'s golden path.*

SIR ISAAC *stands on the shore and watches in amazement.*

No… it can't be done!

JACK: I think it can.

He steps.

I reckon I might.

He steps again.

I know I will!

He runs.

ALL: [*chanting*] Jack Hare! Jack Hare! Jack Hare! Jack Hare!
Run as fast as your furry legs will bear!

JACK *runs the golden path…*

Jack Hare! Jack Hare! Jack Hare! Jack Hare!
Run to the sun, now, if you dare!

JACK: I'm running the golden path!

JACK *runs swiftly. He arrives before the* SUN, *his chest puffed and proud.* SIR ISAAC *stands on the shore, stunned.*

TESSA: [*in the hospital*] He makes it! Look, Joe! He made it!

SIR ISAAC: [*in the Celestial World*] Well, I never… All my life I seem to have been only like a boy playing on a seashore, finding a smoother pebble or a prettier shell than ordinary, whilst the great ocean of truth lay all undiscovered before me. Huh.

He bites his apple and wanders away.

The MOON *looks satisfied. She takes her place in her required orbit, smiling.*

JACK *stands before the* SUN. *The* SUN *looms tall and majestic above him.* JACK *can hardly look at the* SUN*'s face as he glows so radiantly.*

SUN: Well? Why have you come here?

JACK: Oh, Majestic Mr Sun. How furtastic to finally meet you. My name is Jack Hare and I have—my goodness, you're big—I have travelled through earth, air, fire and water to face you. Well, not face you, so to speak, because… Well…

SUN: I'm ugly.

JACK: No! No, you're not ugly!

SUN: Then why are you squinting at me?

JACK: Why, because you're radiant, sir, and my eyes aren't equipped to take in the spectacle. You're certainly not ugly.

SUN: Really? I always thought I was.

JACK: Well, everyone always thought I was stupid and lazy, but now here I am standing in front of you, about to complete my mission and I couldn't have done that without some braves and brainery.

SUN: Your mission?

JACK: [*clearing his throat*] Great Lord Sun, I bring you a precious gift from a noble and gracious lady, and with it comes a rid…

He searches his satchel for the amulet.

Uh… 'tis the finest gift in all the universe and my Lady hath declared it…

He continues to search.

Son of a beehive! Uh… just give me a minute…

He looks around, panicked.

[*To himself*] I've lost it… I must have dropped it somewhere…

SUN: Well?

JACK *swallows nervously.*

JACK: Great lord Sun. I bring you a precious gift from a noble and gracious lady, and it *would* be yours... if it were not the answer to this riddle:

> JACK *sings:*
>
> Fifty is my first...
>
> *The* SUN *thinks for a moment.*
>
> *He traces the air with his golden fingers. He makes an 'L'. This, and the following letters, are projected in sunlit writing around the stage.*
>
> Nothing is my second...
>
> *The* SUN *circles an 'O'.*
>
> A snake will make my third...
>
> *The* SUN *writes an 'S'.*
>
> Then three parts a cross is reckoned...
>
> *Then a 'T'.*
>
> Now to find my name, fit my parts together...
> I am all your past, and you fear me in cold weather.
>
> *The word 'LOST' glows. The* SUN *looks at it sadly.*

That's where your precious gift is, Mr Sun. I'm so sorry.

> *The* SUN *walks away slowly. The word 'LOST' fades away and the stage dims, leaving just* JACK *alone in limbo.*
>
> *A long moment of silence. Then...*

JACK / TESSA: The Sun set and the day was over.

> *Blackness.*

SCENE SIXTEEN

JOE: What?

> TESSA *flips the page of the book.*

TESSA: No. That can't be the end.

JOE: But the Sun doesn't know how much the Moon loves him yet. Jack said the wrong riddle! He was supposed to say:

'Fifty is my first,
Nothing is my second,
Five just makes my third,
My fourth a vowel is reckoned...'

TESSA: No, that's definitely the last line of the book... 'The Sun set and the day was over.' Well, of all the—

JOE: So where is the jewel? Where did Jack lose it?

TESSA: Bloody writers! What a way to end a book!

JOE: The jewel, Mum! Where is it?

TESSA: I don't know.

JOE: So the Sun never gets to know how loved he is?

TESSA looks at JOE sadly.

TESSA: It doesn't seem so. I'm sorry.

Beat. JOE looks away.

JOE: Then I give up.

Beat.

TESSA: Don't you say that.

JOE: I'm not getting better, Mum.

TESSA: You don't know that.

JOE: And it's because of you. You're the one keeping me here. Giving me bad dreams. Reading me books with horrible endings. It's you. You're the worst mortal in the world, Mum.

TESSA: Stop it.

JOE: I mean it. Don't come near me. I give up. And so should you.

TESSA: *Fine!* If that's what you want, then I give up too.

She hurls the book.

SCENE SEVENTEEN

JACK *stands quivering in front of the* MOON.

MOON: You *what?!*

JACK: I... I... I...

MOON: You *lost* it?

JACK: It was so hard to hold onto, mistress Moon. Everyone wanted it.

MOON: But you saw my lord the Sun!

JACK: Yes. Sort of. Had to squint.
MOON: And did you tell him the riddle?
JACK: Yes. Sort of. Had to change it a bit.
MOON: But does he know I love him?
JACK: *That's* the word I was looking for! No. He doesn't. Is that bad?

> *The* MOON *is distraught.*

I take it that's bad.
MOON: You are as small-brained as I thought.
JACK: Not small. Sensibly com—
MOON: Jack Hare, I gave you one task and that was to deliver the amulet to my Lord the Sun and tell him I love him.
JACK: That's two tasks. Really. Isn't it?
MOON: You have lost the amulet and I have lost my love. You are forever banished. As long as that jewel is lost, you no longer exist in this world. You will be forever hidden from the eyes of us all. Go.
JACK: But mistress Moon—
MOON: *Go!*

SCENE EIGHTEEN

JOE *lays in his bed, his back to his mother.*

TESSA *looks out of the window sadly. The* NURSE *enters.*

NURSE: Test results came through. No change.

> *The* NURSE *leaves.*

> TESSA *sings softly:*

TESSA: No change.
No change.
In here there is no change…

How can I be jealous of a simple grey hare
Who gets to see the world on a passionate dare?
Why do the Moon and Sun, painted on a page,
Get to be so full of love while I'm so full of rage?
Where is the colour in my life? Where is the joy?
Why am I imprisoned with my sick little boy?

Why is it always me that has to be strong?
When all I really want to do is curl up with my mum?
Where are all my friends? How did this come to be?
Who am I to this child? Who am I to me?
Why can't I greet the dawn from some sandy seashore,
And dance with new people or even break the law?
But…
I can't help but wonder…
Is this my eternity? Is this my forever?
Am I here to be forgotten? Is this the start of never?
My world is one big riddle that I just can't figure out,
A story with no ending is all my life's about.

But it must change.
It must change.
It must change for us in here.

Just to live one day as that lucky little hare.

TESSA *is breathless, invigorated. She turns to see* JOE *watching on, wide-eyed. She walks back to him determinedly.*

Come on, Joe. We're going to find that jewel.

JOE *nods and takes her hand.*

END OF ACT ONE

ACT TWO

SCENE ONE

A BAND MEMBER *is a lone figure on the stage. They play a melody introducing us to our next adventure ...*

JACK *appears on the other side of the stage, in a cage.*

JACK *sings forlornly.*

JACK: I'm not the kind who gets to have a title,
 I'm not the kind who's looked upon with awe,
 I'm not the kind who gets to rule the jungle,
 For that you need a quite impressive roar.

He roars weakly, then coughs.

I'm not the kind who gets to rule the ocean,
The water soaks my furry coat right through,
I'm not the kind who deals that well with fire,
Especially if I end up in a stew.

But everyone deserves to be noticed
For the little things they bring into the world,
I didn't mean to stuff it up
When I lost the amulet,
But now I'm here, invisible to all.

The MOON *appears and sings.*

MOON: I'm not the kind who ever stays in one place,
 I much prefer to wax and to wane,
 I'm not the kind who feels they have to linger.
 I come and go—it's just my little game.

But everyone deserves to be noticed
For the little things they bring into the world,
I know it mightn't seem that hard
To live here in the sky of stars,
But I feel I'm invisible to all.

The SUN *appears and sings.*

SUN: I am the kind that people take for granted,
They know I'm going to rise up every day,
I'm not the kind to ruin expectations,
But sometimes it's in bed I'd rather stay.

Cos everyone deserves to be noticed
For the little things they bring into the world,
But if I shine too bright they block the light,
If my smile's too wide they run inside,
So I feel like I'm invisible to all.

JACK: Oh, I feel I'm invisible to all…
MOON: Yes, I feel I'm invisible to all…
SUN: Oh, I feel I'm invisible to all…
MOON / JACK: I feel like I'm invisible…
ALL: I'm really just invisible to all.

SCENE TWO

TESSA *and* JOE *stand on the seashore.* JOE *wears his pyjama bottoms and ugg boots.* TESSA *wears her usual dress. Wispy clouds float overhead in the pre-dawn sky.* TESSA *and* JOE *stare at the sky.*

TESSA: How are you feeling, Joe?
JOE: Much better, actually. I'll be glad when the Sun's up.
TESSA: Likewise. We're going to find his jewel for him.

The SUN *is dozing.* TESSA *calls out in his general direction.*

Did you hear that, sir? My name is Tessa. My son Joe and I have travelled a long way to be here. We've broken a lot of rules. We're probably in a lot of trouble. But we're going to find your lost jewel.

She waves. JOE *does too.*

A WOMAN *in a gold swimming suit and a swimming cap appears. She gazes out across the water.*

DAWN: Dawn.
TESSA: Yes. Beautiful.
DAWN: Thank you. I keep myself in good shape.
TESSA: Pardon?

DAWN: Oh, sorry. My name's Dawn. How do you do?
TESSA: Oh! Well, thank you. I'm Tessa. This is my son Joe.
DAWN: You're not from around here, are you?
TESSA: Not really, no.
JOE: We're looking for lost treasure.
DAWN: Of course you are.
JOE: We're going to find the amulet that Jack Hare lost. Then we're going to give it to the Sun and tell him the Moon loves him.
DAWN: Really? That's quite an adventure.
JOE / TESSA: I know.
JOE: Do you know him? The Sun?
DAWN: Know him? We're related, somewhere along the line. Most people are around these parts.
TESSA: Would you know the best place to start looking for the jewel?
DAWN: I always think it's best to keep the subject of inquiry constantly before me, and wait till the first dawning opens gradually, little by little, into a full and clear light. Don't you?

> DAWN *smiles at* TESSA. TESSA *looks back, strangely.* THE MAN WHO PLAYS THE MUSIC THAT MAKES THE WORLD GO ROUND *appears and starts to play softly.* TESSA *smiles at* DAWN.

TESSA: Thank you. That's very… helpful. Can you point us in the right direction, please?

> DAWN *raises her hand and points away from the sea.* TESSA *grins and gathers her things. She calls to* JOE.

Come on, Joe. We've got to start searching!

> JOE *hurries after her.*

Thank you, Dawn! Have a nice day!
DAWN: I always, always do.

SCENE THREE

TESSA *and* JOE *walk through a town along a quiet street.*

JOE: Are you sure we're supposed to be here, Mum? It's kind of creepy.
TESSA: Just keep your eyes peeled, Joe. Jack could have dropped the amulet anywhere.

ACT TWO

A tune begins. A really, really bad BARBERSHOP QUARTET. *Only there's only three of them. They stand at a store nearby called the 'Hare-Do Barber Shop'. An old barbershop pole sits beside the shop with a hare weathervane on top. The* BARBERS *enthusiastically sing a cappella.*

BARBERS: We are the hare-do barbers,
We really do do hair,
We are the hare-do barbers,
For hair we greatly care.

If you require a number one
Or you're looking for a nice tight bun,
We are the hare-do barbers,
We really do do hair,
We are the hare-do barbers,
For hair we greatly care.

Just step inside, right this way
For a nice tight curl or a firm toupee,
We are the hare-do barbers,
We really do do hair,
We are the hare-do barbers,
For hair we greatly care.

We are the hare-do barbeeeeeeeeeeeers…

They hold the note for an abnormally long time. TESSA *and* JOE *just watch on, confused. The* BARBERS *hold the note, their faces practically turning blue until finally* TESSA *and* JOE *make their way over to the barber store. The relieved* BARBERS *finally continue their song.*

We really do do hair.

The BARBERS *wait expectantly for applause.* TESSA *and* JOE *reluctantly oblige. They bow to* TESSA *and* JOE.

BARBER BOB: Welcome, welcome! We are the Hare-Do Barbershop Quartet. I'm Barber Bob.
BARBER BILL: I'm Barber Bill.
BARBER BARBARA: And I'm Barber Barbara.

Sam Martin, Phil Moriarty and Guy Freer as the Barbers in Griffin Theatre Company and State Theatre Company of South Australia's 2015 production at the Sydney Opera House. (Photo: Brett Boardman)

They all grin broadly. JOE *and* TESSA *look confused.*

JOE: Where's the other one?
BARBERS: Pardon?
JOE: I think 'quartet' means 'four'. If you're a Barbershop Quartet, then shouldn't there be four of you?

The BARBERS *look uncomfortable.*

BARBER BARBARA: You mean Ali.
BARBER BILL: Ali Barber. He was our fourth member. We lost him a little while back.
TESSA: Oh, we're very sorry. Was it sudden?
BARBER BOB: Yes. One minute he was here, the next he was working for a topiary company a few miles east. Now he cuts hedges instead of hair. Tragic loss to our business.
BARBER BARBARA: It'll pick up soon.
BARBER BILL: Barber Barbara, you haven't had any customers in so long your scissors have rusted shut.
TESSA: Well, there's not many people out there who can sing while they snip. I'd love to have my hair cut by you.
BARBER BARBARA: Really?!
BARBER BOB: Well, you should have said so earlier!

They start fiddling with TESSA*'s hair and preparing their scissors.*

TESSA: Uh, no… please. That's… that's not what / I meant.
BARBER BARBARA: Look at these split ends!
BARBER BILL: Yes, you're setting a terrible example for your son here.

TESSA *and* JOE *are both shoved into barber chairs.* JOE *holds tight to his beanie.*

TESSA: No, please—we really must be on our way—
BARBER BOB: Come on, little man. Let's take a look, shall we?
JOE: Please don't touch my head!
BARBER BOB: Nonsense! There's nothing to be afraid of! We just want to see your—

He whips off the beanie to reveal JOE*'s bald head. The* BARBERS *all recoil in shock.*

BARBERS: —hair.

JOE *looks terribly embarrassed.*

JOE: I… don't have any.

> TESSA *snatches the beanie back from* BARBER BARBARA *and places it on* JOE's *head. The* BARBERS *look at one another, ashamed. They get into a little huddle and whisper to one another. Then* BARBER BOB *brings out a large cage on wheels, covered by a cloth.*

BARBER BOB: [*sung*] If you don't have any hair to spare, then please allow us to—

ALL: Spare our haaaaaaare!

> *He whips off the cloth to reveal* JACK, *who is sound asleep.*

JOE: Mum! It's Jack!

TESSA: Jack Hare! *The* Jack Hare?!

JOE: Where did you find him?

BARBER BILL: We didn't. He just turned up here one day, in that cage, with a sign saying…

BARBER BARBARA: 'Unwanted Hare'.

BARBER BOB: We specialise in unwanted hairs, so this is where he ended up.

JOE: It *is* Jack Hare! Mum, can we keep him? He might be able to help us find the jewel.

TESSA: Well, he was the one that lost it. Alright. [*To the* BARBERS] Thank you.

BARBER BARBARA: Is there anything else we can help you with?

TESSA: As a matter of fact, there is. We're looking for a lost treasure. We think it might have been dropped around here somewhere. It looks… [*looking at* JACK] well, a little like him, but it is adorned with all the jewels of the earth. Have you seen it?

> *The* BARBERS *shake their heads.*

BARBER BILL: There's only one man in this town who knows about jewels and treasures and all things lost and found and that's the Practical Man.

JACK: [*mumbling*] The Practical Man…

BARBER BARBARA: The Practical Man…

JACK: [*mumbling*] The Practical Man…

ACT TWO 43

BARBER BOB: The Practical Man…

He indicates the nearby antiquities store. It looks a lot more run-down than the last time we saw it—grubby and dilapidated. Some of its windows are boarded up and the 'ANTIQUITIES' signage has faded, apart from the letters 'QUIT'. JOE *and* TESSA *gasp.*

Suddenly, JACK *wakes with a start.*

JACK: Don't burn me bum! Please don't burn me bum!

He runs around the cage wildly. The BARBERS *have wiped their hands clean of the hare and go back into their store.* JACK *continues screaming and ranting until he finally settles down— but only when he sees* JOE'*s bald head.*

Where's your hair?

JOE: I beg your pardon.

JACK: Your hair. Where's your hair?

JOE: Well… you're my hare.

JACK: How can I be your hair? I'm not the right colour, for a start. I'd look completely weird sitting on top of *your* head.

They both look at one another strangely. JOE *realises his beanie is off.*

JOE: Oh! Oh, no, no, no.

He replaces his beanie hurriedly.

Not *this* hair. Hare. As in rabbit. As in you. You're my hare. The hare I've heard so much about. I'm Joe.

JACK: Technically, I'm not a rabbit. Rabbits are pests and have rather a bad reputation for… Well, I can't go into it. You're just a boy. But I've been banished to this cage, so I certainly haven't been getting up to that kind of business, although there was that moment with a Playboy Bunny a few years back— What do you mean you've heard about me?

JOE: We read about you and the amulet you lost.

JACK: That thwapping amulet. You'll never find it. It's been lost for years. And if *I* couldn't complete the journey, then I don't know how a mortal could. Now go home and grow some hair. Leave me alone. I'm busy.

JOE *tries again.*

JOE: Me and my mum—

TESSA: My mum and I.

JOE: My mum and I want to find that amulet and give it to its rightful owner the Sun so that he knows the Moon loves him.

JACK: You've brought your mum along?! What are you, scared? Need mummy to hold your paw?! Pfft. I never took my mummy. Not that I could. Pie filling. Terrible end. But I'm not joining some bald child and his mortal mother on a pointless treasure hunt for—

He catches sight of TESSA.

Well, helloooo!

JACK *is obviously enamoured.*

You must be Joe's mum. You are radishing.

TESSA: A pleasure to meet you too, Jack Hare. We're searching for the amulet you lost. We thought you might like to help us.

JACK: Always happy to assist a beautiful lady. Now, if you'll just open this cage, I'll be at your peck and ball.

TESSA: Wonderful.

She goes to unlock the cage.

Our first stop is to speak with the Practical Man.

JACK *has a complete nervous breakdown. It lasts quite some time. When he's done...*

Jack, are you afraid of the Practical Man?

JACK *quivers.*

What if I were to hold your paw the whole time? Would that make it less scary?

JACK *thinks.*

JACK: Hold me paw?

TESSA *nods.*

You?

TESSA *nods.*

Deal. Get me out of this fuzzin' cage.

JACK takes some time to get out of the cage. TESSA *holds his paw.*

JACK*'s leg quivers.*

As the set rotates there is a moment of calm and then...

SCENE FOUR

The Practical Man's shop appears.

PRACTICAL MAN: Ah! Ah... step in! Step in!

JACK *screams and hides.*

I have many, uh... treasures of antiquity that will fake your tancy.

Beat.

Uh... take your fancy.

He peers at JACK *who is quivering nearby.*

Have we met before?

JACK *quivers fearfully.* TESSA *holds his paw tight.*

TESSA: We don't want to take up too much of your time—
PRACTICAL MAN: Oh, my stars! Not at all! Wonderful to have your custom.
TESSA: We're looking for a rather special jewel.
PRACTICAL MAN: A special jewel? Well, you've come to exactly the right place. Let me see. So many special, special, special jewels.
JACK: Probably all stolen from poor defenceless lagomorphs.

JOE *looks confused.*

That's me scientifical name. Do you know any big words?
JOE: Umm... Haemoglobin. Chemotherapy. Radical nephrectomy.
JACK: Oooh! 'Radical neck-recto-flea'. Little show-off.

The PRACTICAL MAN *rifles madly through his pockets.*

PRACTICAL MAN: Here we are! Beautiful necklace.
JOE: That's a piece of string.

He rifles again.

PRACTICAL MAN: Spectacular earrings?

He places pegs on his ears.

TESSA: They're clothes pegs.

PRACTICAL MAN: [*pointing*] Oh, look! A thing!

As they turn to look, he stomps on a dead cockroach. They turn back.

Magnificent brooch!

TESSA / JOE: Dead cockroach.

JACK: Oooh. I'll have that. Thanks.

He eats it. Everyone looks repulsed.

What?

JOE: Please… we're looking for an amulet.

The PRACTICAL MAN's *smile fades.*

PRACTICAL MAN: An amulet, you say?

TESSA, JOE *and* JACK *nod.* TESSA *points to* JACK.

TESSA: Yes. Looks a little bit like him, but sparkly.

PRACTICAL MAN: Ah, yes, I know that jewel. I once held it in my hands. I was so close… and then…

JACK: You tried to steal it by pushing me in the fire.

PRACTICAL MAN: I did no such thing!

JACK: You did! Look at me bum!

He shows him his bum which is singed black.

PRACTICAL MAN: Alright, I did. I did.

He starts to sob.

Oh, what kind of man am I?! I used to be the finest antiquities salesman in all the region and now I'm selling cockroaches as jewellery. I *was* The Practical Man and now I'm wearing pegs on my ears. And they really hurt! What's practical about that?!

He sobs. JACK *is sobbing too. He and the* PRACTICAL MAN *fall into an embrace.*

JACK: There, there, you silly sausage. The good thing about being the Practical Man means you can be practically anything. I'm sure things will look up for you very soon.

ACT TWO

The PRACTICAL MAN *sniffles.*

PRACTICAL MAN: Thank you. I'm sorry I burnt your pantaloons.

JACK: Knickerbockers.

The PRACTICAL MAN *whistles the tune as he departs.* TESSA *hears and joins in as they leave the store…*

TESSA: Fifty is my first,
Nothing is my second,
Five just makes my third…

JACK joins in, quickening the pace.

TESSA / JACK: My fourth, a vowel is reckoned…

JOE *joins in.*

ALL: Now to find my name,
Fit my parts together,
I die if I get cold,
But never fear cold weather.

SCENE FIVE

THE MAN WHO PLAYS THE MUSIC THAT MAKES THE WORLD GO ROUND *enters, playing an upbeat melody. He is accompanied by a dancing* FAT PIG.

JACK: Hallo, The Man Who Plays the Music That Makes the World Go Round!

THE MAN: Hello, Jack!

JACK: May I introduce the absolutely betwitching Tessa and her son Joe. They're my new friends.

The FAT PIG *snuffles again and wriggles wildly.*

TESSA: Excuse me—is your pig alright?

THE MAN: Oh, she's fine. It's the power of music, you see. Not only can I make the world go round with it, but I can also conjure up laughter, melancholy and tears. Do you know when you've had a good day? It's usually because I'm playing this song.

He plays some more of the melody.

JOE: It is a very happy tune.

THE MAN: Yes—but hear this… This is what I'm usually playing when you have a bad day.

> *He plays a mournful tune. The mood shifts. The* FAT PIG *dances sorrowfully.* TESSA, JOE *and* JACK'S *smiles fade.*

TESSA: Please play something else. We've had enough of bad days. Make us laugh.

THE MAN: A tune for laughing? Very well!

> THE MAN *plays a tune of laughter, complete with comic faces and tricks with his bow. He starts to sing:*

> Crotchets and quavers and beats and rhyme,
> These are things that keep the time,
> These are things that keep the beat,
> Things that will make you tap your feet.

The FAT PIG *taps her feet.*

> Semiquavers dancing through a tune
> Can make a dish run away with a spoon,
> Melodies filled with joy and romance,
> Things that will make you get up and dance.

JACK *and* TESSA *begin to dance.*

> The music I play on my violin
> Makes the world turn, helps it to spin,
> It can make a pig dance, it can help love bloom,
> The earth pirouettes at the sound of my tune.

By now everyone is dancing wildly and joyfully.

> There's only one rule I have to heed
> In this song of joy, this song of glee,
> That every so often without warning
> I have to stop my violin.

He stops abruptly. Everyone halts mid-dance. THE MAN *hangs his head.*

Silence.

The FAT PIG *weeps softly.*

JOE: [*whispering*] Why has he stopped playing, Mum?

ACT TWO

TESSA: I don't know.

They wait a little longer. THE MAN *continues to hang his head. The* FAT PIG *continues to weep.*

JACK: When he stops playing, the world loses one of its mortals.

TESSA: What? That's terrible!

JACK: He is The Man Who Plays the Music That Makes the World Go Round. Part of making the world go round is allowing some people to hop off now and then.

TESSA: But how does he know when to stop playing?

THE MAN *finally raises his head.*

THE MAN: Usually at a page turn or after a long-held note. Or whenever I play D-flat. But of all these years doing it, the world always starts to turn again when I play once more. Some of the remaining mortals become a little slower, a little sadder—for them the world still feels like it's stopped—but they soon hear the music I play and pick up the pace once again.

He begins to play again. A pleasant, steady song.

JOE: Do you decide which mortal has to stop dancing?

THE MAN: No. I just keep the time.

TESSA: We're looking for a treasure of lost love.

JACK: *That word again! It's infurriating!*

THE MAN: Ahhh… the famous amulet that Jack lost.

JACK: I wish people would stop harping on about that.

JOE: That's the one. Have you seen it?

THE MAN: A long, long time ago. I must have played a billion notes since that day.

JOE *begins to cough a little.* TESSA *looks up at him worriedly.*

TESSA: We're searching for it. It's rather urgent. We… don't have much time.

THE MAN *holds out his stopwatch.*

THE MAN: For you.

JOE: But it's your stopwatch. How are you going to keep time without it?

THE MAN: The music keeps time for me. Take it. Please. You need it more than I do.

He smiles gently at TESSA. JOE *takes the watch.* JACK *takes it from* JOE *and inspects it.*

JOE: Thank you. Do you know the way to the Sun?

THE MAN: Shh. He's watching, you know.

He points his bow directly up. The SUN *stares down at them from above. They all squint back at him.*

He always sits up there at this time of day. Watching over all of us. Making sure we're on the right track.

JACK: I met him once. Strange fellow. Thinks the whole world revolves around him.

TESSA: What time is it?

THE MAN *looks up at the* SUN, JACK *looks at the watch.*

THE MAN / TESSA: Midday.

JACK: Twelve.

TESSA: Goodness. Time's running away from us. How did it get so late?

JOE: Come on, Mum. We have to hurry. Goodbye, Fat Pig! Goodbye, The Man Who Plays the Music That Makes the World Go Round! Please stay awake a little longer, Mr Sun! We have something we want to find for you.

JOE *hurries off with* JACK. TESSA *follows but then turns back to* THE MAN.

TESSA: Keep playing for as long as you can. For us.

THE MAN *smiles, then closes his eyes and plays on.* TESSA *leaves.*

SCENE SIX

TARA *suddenly lands on them all with an inelegant thud. She carries a large sack with her.*

TARA: Perfect landing. Hallo there, Jack! I heard you were banished! Nice to see you round the traps again.

JACK: Traps? Where?

He looks around worriedly.

JOE: You're Tara Treetops!

ACT TWO 51

TARA: Indeed. And this is my friend Craw.
CRAW: Craw! Craw!
TARA: And you must be Joe…

She shakes TESSA*'s hand.*

CRAW: Joe!
TARA: … and Tessa.

She shakes JOE*'s hand.*

CRAW: Tessa!
JOE: Actually, I'm—
TARA: Joe. Meaning 'He Will Add'. Tessa. Meaning 'Gatherer'.
TESSA: Well, fingers crossed. We're hoping we might gather more information as to the whereabouts of Jack's lost amulet. Have you seen it at all?
JACK: You remember it, Tara—the one I was delivering to the Sun.
CRAW: The one he lost! The one he lost!
JACK: Stop saying that!
CRAW: Bossy pants! Bossy pants!
JACK: They're *knickerbockers*!
TARA: Funny you should mention that. I've been out looking for lost dreams and my sack is full of amulet fancies.
JOE: Really?

TARA *rifles through her bag and pulls out lost dreams.*

TARA: Yes! Let's see. There's one here from a Henry and another from a Lee. Here's a lost amulet dream from a Dunisha. Another from a Maisie.
JOE: Are we in there?
TARA: Ahh… Nope. That's it.

JOE *and* TESSA *look crestfallen.*

Why so glum? This is a sack of *lost* dreams. If your dreams aren't in here, that means *you* still have them. And they're the best dreams of all.
CRAW: Best dreams! Best dreams!
JACK: My best dream is this… I smell something under the earth, and using my keen and brilliant sense of olfactory fabulousness, I pinpoint exactly where it is buried, and I dig and I dig and I dig

and my fur gets all soiled and muddy but I don't care, I just keep digging deeper and deeper and deeper, following the smell, until there—right in front of me—is—wait for it—the world's biggest, fattest, orangest, deliciousest-est-est carrot. And it's all mine and no-one else's and every time I take a bite out of it it grows back again. It's like an infinite carrot. An infinite! Carrot! Best. Dream. Ever.

> *Beat.*

Sometimes when I wake up I'm chewing my own foot.

TESSA: Well, my best dream is a nice hot shower followed by a cup of tea brewed in my very own kitchen and then a long sleep.

JACK / TARA: Pfft. Bor-ing!

JACK: Where's the carrot?!

TARA: What's your best dream, Joe?

JOE: I'm... not sure.

JACK: Come on. You must have a best dream somewhere.

JOE: Um... Well...

> *Everyone looks at* JOE *expectantly.*
>
> JOE *sings, a little tentatively at first.*
>
>> I dream of outside.
>>
>> Slippery wet grass that cuts at my feet,
>> Splinters in fingers and scabs on my knees,
>> Chasing fat beetles, getting stung by a bee.
>>
>> I dream of outside.

JACK: And carrots?

JOE: I dream of food.

>> Crunchy potatoes and big juicy steaks,
>> Cauliflower cheese piled high on my plate,
>> Crumpets with honey and caramel cake.
>>
>> I dream—

JACK: Of carrots!

JOE: I dream of running.

>> Running as fast and as free as I dare,
>> Feeling the breeze whipping through my hair,

          I don't know where I'm going and I don't even care.
          I dream of running.
JACK: With carrots…
JOE: I dream of playing.
          Of wrestling with friends till we're bruised and we're sore,
          And I fart on their heads till they scream, 'No more!'
          Of catching and chasing and toppling and tumbling and racing and not keeping score.

          I dream of playing.
JACK: With carrots…
JOE: I dream of home.
          Hearing Mum sing as she brews her tea,
          Smelling hot toast that I know is for me,
          Not needing nurses to help me wee.
JOE / TESSA: I dream of home.
JOE: I dream of green frogs and stubbing my toes,
          And how snow must feel when it falls on your nose,
          And going to school and learning my tables,
          And Grimms' fairy tales and Aesop's fables,
TARA: And how someday I'd like to speak Japanese,
JOE: And say sorry to Billy, who I used to tease,
          And write to my dad to say it's okay,
TESSA: And I hope you see him again one day,
JOE: I'd like to ride a curling wave,
          And grow a moustache just so I can shave,
          And help out the people much sicker than me,
          And I'd love to try to train a flea,
          And just once I'd like to chew bubble gum
          (I know it's bad for my teeth though, Mum),
          And I'd like to go on a flying fox,
          And have my own pair of Superman jocks,
          And one day I'll own my own talking parrot,
          And I'll help Jack Hare as he digs for carrots.
JACK: *Finally!*
JOE: And… That's all… Yes, that's it, for now, it seems…
          But I'm sure I'll add to my list of best dreams.

TARA: Well, it was scientifically proven recently that for every bad dream a person has, they have four hundred and seventy-nine best ones. Hang on tight to all of them, I say. Every dream has a message. Especially the ones about missing amulets.

TESSA: Well, we've looked everywhere for it. In the sky, in the ocean, we've asked every manner of creature that walks the earth...

TARA: Ah, but have you looked beneath it? If I can't see it from up there, and you can't find it down here, then it must be buried deep in the earth. Somewhere round the traps.

JACK: *Buried* traps?! My Uncle Trevor went that way. Terrible.

TARA: Goodbye, Joe!

She shakes TESSA's *hand.*

CRAW: Goodbye, Joe!

TARA: Goodbye, Tessa!

She shakes JOE's *hand.*

CRAW: Goodbye, Tessa!

TARA: Goodbye, Jack Hare! Good luck with your search. And hang onto your dreams or they'll end up in my sack. Ally-oop!

TARA and CRAW fly wildly away.

SCENE SEVEN

JOE *begins to cough. He looks weaker than ever.*

JACK: Tessa...

TESSA: Yes, Jack?

JACK: Is Joe alright? He looks a bit funny. Gone a strange colour.

TESSA: He's fine. He's fine. You're alright, Joe, aren't you?

JOE nods and gives a weak smile.

JOE: It's been a long day. My eyes are a bit tired.

JACK: It's not myxomatosis, is it? My cousin Jessica went that way. Nasty. Her eyes went bright pink, right, and then this weird stuff started to ooze—

TESSA: Joe? Do you want to—?

JOE: No, Mum. Let's keep going.

But his cough worsens. He sits on the ground weakly.

ACT TWO

PENNY *enters.* JACK *hides behind her skirt.*

PENNY: That's a nasty cough. Serves you right for wandering about in only your pyjamas at this time of day.

JOE: What time is it?

PENNY: Almost dusk.

TESSA: Already?

JOE: That's when the Sun begins to close his eyes. Mum! We have to hurry!

TESSA: I know, Joe. We will. Pardon me, miss.

PENNY: Mzzzzz.

TESSA: Sorry. Mzzzzz… Penny Pockets.

PENNY: How do you know my name?

TESSA: Your wares are so renowned.

PENNY: My wares? Really?

TESSA: Your honey, in particular, is world famous.

JACK: It's not that good.

PENNY: Shut your trap.

JACK: Traps!

He screams and hides under PENNY*'s dress.*

PENNY: My honey is the best.

TESSA: I was wondering if you'd allow my son a taste. We're on a very important journey and he hasn't eaten for quite some time.

PENNY: Ten dollars.

TESSA: Pardon?

PENNY: Actually, no, thirteen.

TESSA: Wait, I—

PENNY: Fifteen.

TESSA: No, you don't understand—

PENNY: You've got a sick boy there. A good mother would pay any price to see her son well.

TESSA: Of course, but—

PENNY: Twenty dollars.

TESSA: I don't have any—

PENNY: Came out without your purse, hey?

TESSA: Yes!

PENNY: A likely story. Twenty-five.

TESSA: You drive a very hard bargain, Ms Pockets.
PENNY: [*singing*]
>A good mother will always have her purse
>To show her child exactly what they're worth,
>A good mother will always have the money
>To pay for things like toys and trucks and honey.

>A good mother will always have the coins
>To shower on the sweet fruit of her loins,
>A good mother would hock her very locket
>To spare the shame of having empty pockets.

>But a bad mother will talk of things like love,
>She'll kiss her child and cover him with hugs,
>She'll pretend that such displays of affection
>Can replace the fact a child should be spoilt rotten!

>A good mother…

TESSA: Let me just have a look…

She searches her pockets.

PENNY: A bad mother…
TESSA: I might have something tucked away in here…
PENNY: A good mother…
TESSA: If you could just give me a little more time…
PENNY: A bad mother…
TESSA: Must be in my other coat…

TESSA desperately searches her pockets for change.

During the song, JACK has been pinching from PENNY's pockets as JOE watches on, laughing softly.

JACK reaches a furry paw up into PENNYs pockets and pilfers a piece of honeycomb. He gives it to JOE who chomps down on it hungrily.

PENNY: But a good mother will lay out the cash,
>A good mother will always have a stash,
>A good mother will not be so hard wrought,
>A good mother will know that love can be bought…

JACK has emptied PENNY's pockets. TESSA looks at PENNY helplessly, her own pockets just as empty.

… for two million, seven hundred thousand and eleventeen dollars. That's my final price.

She waits for TESSA to answer. TESSA stands defeated.

No? Bye-bye!

PENNY sashays off, leaving TESSA looking completely shattered.

Beat.

JOE: It's okay, Mum. I feel much better now.

TESSA shakes her head sadly.

TESSA: I'm sorry, Joe. I don't have any money. I never have and I probably never will.

JACK: Now, now, Tessa. Don't you listen to that nasty lady.

JACK trips and the goods go flying.

TESSA: Jack, where on earth did you get all of those things?

JACK: From Penny Pockets' pockets.

TESSA: You stole them?

JACK: Borrowed! Let's not split hares!

TESSA's not amused. JACK tries another tack.

I was going to give them back! She took off before I could replace them!

JOE approaches TESSA and holds out the honeycomb.

JOE: Here, Mum. Eat something.

TESSA hesitates, then takes it and eats ravenously. Between mouthfuls…

TESSA: Alright. Just this once. But stealing is wrong, Joe. And Jack, I expect you to return all of these to Penny Pockets. She's a businesswoman. And they're rightfully hers. Except this, of course. Which is delicious.

She keeps eating.

JACK: Joe! Look! It's my mistress!

SCENE EIGHT

The MOON *enters and a dim light rises. She looks sad and wild and sings a haunting melody.*

JOE: [*whispering*] Mum... it's her. The Moon.

    They watch as she meanders strangely.

JACK: Mistress, you don't look at all well. Mistress? Can you hear me? It's your devoted servant Jack Hare. Mistress?

TESSA: She can't see you, Jack. She's lovesick.

JACK: Laaahhhhve-sick?

TESSA: The only one she's looking out for is her Sun.

    Across the stage, the SUN *sees the* MOON. *She begins to dance for him. He watches. They hold out their hands and walk toward one another.*

    JACK, JOE *and* TESSA *watch. The light continues to shift. The* MOON *and the* SUN *smile at one another longingly as they get closer and closer... but only as close as they are prescribed to by the Laws of the Universe.*

    The light turns to dusk.

    TESSA *holds* JOE *close to her.*

    A beat, then...

SCENE NINE

JOE *turns to* TESSA.

JOE: This is it, Mum. This is the place where Jack dropped the jewel. I can feel it. There. It's there. Like Tara Treetops said, it's buried beneath the earth.

    They hone in on a spot...

    The SUN *starts to turn away from the* MOON *and the light fades a little.*

TESSA: Then quick! Start digging!

    TESSA *digs madly as* JOE *and Jack watch on.*

JOE: *I'm sure this is the place, Mum!*

> TESSA *continues digging at the ground, deeper and deeper, tearing at the earth. The* SUN *disappears completely.*
>
> JOE *looks frail and unwell. He sits on the ground and watches* TESSA *dig frantically.* TESSA *does not notice.*

TESSA: No.

> *She searches the soil.*

This can't be right.

> *She looks around frantically.*

We've come so far!

> *She begins to sob.*

Why isn't it here?! Where has it gone?! *No!*

> *She looks devastated.*

I'm so sorry, Joe. It really is lost.

> *Beat.*

JOE: Mum! It doesn't matter.

> JOE *starts singing the riddle.* TESSA *goes to him.*
>
> Fifty is my first…
>
> *The* SUN *reappears…*

JACK: The Sun has come back!

JOE: Nothing is my second…

> *The* MOON *appears across the stage…*

JACK: And my mistress the Moon!

JOE: Five just makes my third,
    My fourth, a vowel is reckoned…

ALL: Now to find my name,
    Fit my parts together,
    I die if I get cold,
    But never fear cold weather…

> *Everyone watches as the* SUN *and the* MOON *break all laws of the universe.* JACK, *stunned, stands between them.*

The MOON *and the* SUN *each kiss a cheek of* JACK*'s. It is a lingering kiss of love to each other, via the hare, that illuminates the entire universe and the furry messenger.*

JOE *smiles.*

JOE: Mum… I love you.

TESSA: Pfft. Soppy.

They embrace. JACK *watches the* SUN *and the* MOON *and the mother and her son.*

JACK: Love.

A beat. He gets it. He gasps.

Love! I can say it! I can say it! *Love!* Love is… feeling funny in your belly. Love is your leg jumping up and down when someone strokes your paw. Love is feeling happier than Larry, whoever he is. Love is your heart beating your brain in a race. Love happens even if you have no hair, no money, no hare and no honey. Love is the lost dream and the found dream, the bad dreams and the best dreams. Love is a mother and her son and a son and his mum and the moon and the sun and everything in between.

He turns to the others.

Joe loves his mum! Tessa loves Joe! I love Tessa! The Man Who Plays the Music That Makes the World Go Round loves his Pig! His Pig loves him right back! I love carrots! We all love someone! Even you, Penny Pockets!

PENNY: Not really.

THE BARBERS: We love yooou!

PENNY: Really? Naaaaaaw …

JACK: My mistress the Moon loves the Sun! That's what I was supposed to tell you, sir! Love! The riddle is *love!*

The SUN *beams at the* MOON. *She beams right back at him.*

MOON: Jack Hare.

JACK: Yes, mistress Moon?

MOON: You delivered my message to the Sun. You can come home now.

JACK *leaps excitedly. He turns and grins at* JOE *and* TESSA.

ACT TWO

JACK: *She loves me!* Yeah, yeah, yeah!

> *He goes to leave, but turns to* TESSA *and* JOE *first.*

Goodbye, mortals. Thank you for a lovely day.

> *He kisses* TESSA*'s hand softly and gives* JOE *a cuddle.* JOE *gives* JACK *his beanie.*
>
> JACK *goes to his mistress the* MOON. *She pats him fondly.*
>
> TESSA *smiles. She and* JOE *sit beneath the* SUN, *the* MOON *and the multitude of stars. The sounds of day fill the space and for a long time, the characters sit in its beautiful cacophony.*
>
> THE MAN WHO PLAYS THE MUSIC THAT MAKES THE WORLD GO ROUND *plays the 'Song of the Sun'.*
>
> *As the light fades, so do the sounds, and a gentle stillness arrives, but* THE MAN *keeps playing.*
>
> *A golden path of light leads to* JOE. TESSA *looks down at him in her arms. His eyes are peacefully closed. She strokes his head and kisses him softly.* THE MAN WHO PLAYS THE MUSIC THAT MAKES THE WORLD GO ROUND *puts down his violin bow.*
>
> *Silence.*
>
> TESSA *looks up and speaks to the audience.*

TESSA: The sun set and the day was over.

> *She smiles a smile that has a beauty that is forever, and mocks Time.*
>
> *The lights slowly fade to black as…*
>
> THE MAN WHO PLAYS THE MUSIC THAT MAKES THE WORLD GO ROUND *resumes the steady tune on his violin and* TESSA *holds her little boy.*

THE END

www.currency.com.au

Visit Currency Press' website now to:

- Order books
- Browse through our full list of titles including plays, screenplays, theory and criticism, performance handbooks, educational texts and more
- Choose a play for your school or performance group by cast specs
- Seek performance rights
- Find out about performing arts news
- For students: read our study guides
- For teachers: access free curriculum information and teacher notes

We are also on Facebook and Instagram (@currencypress). Join the conversation!

The performing arts publisher

www.ingramcontent.com/pod-product-compliance
Lightning Source LLC
Chambersburg PA
CBHW050023090426
42734CB00021B/3398